# CAMARASAURUS

## and Other Dinosaurs of the Garden Park Digs in Colorado

by Dougal Dixon

illustrated by
**Steve Weston** and **James Field**

PICTURE WINDOW BOOKS
Minneapolis, Minnesota

Picture Window Books
151 Good Counsel Drive
P.O. Box 669
Mankato, MN 56002-0669
877-845-8392
www.picturewindowbooks.com

Printed in the United States of America.

 All books published by Picture Window Books
are manufactured with paper containing at
least 10 percent post-consumer waste.

**Library of Congress Cataloging-in-Publication Data**
Dixon, Dougal.
Camarasaurus and other dinosaurs of the Garden
Park digs in Colorado / by Dougal Dixon ; illustrated
by Steve Weston and James Fields.
p. cm. – (Dinosaur find)
Includes index.
ISBN 978-1-4048-4717-0 (library binding)
1. Camarasaurus—Juvenile literature. 2. Dinosaurs—
Colorado—Garden Park—Juvenile literature.
3. Paleontology—Colorado—Garden Park—Juvenile
literature. I. Weston, Steve, ill.
II. Field, James, 1959- ill. III. Title.
QE862.S3D5927 2009
567.909788'53—dc22                    2008006348

**Acknowledgments**
This book was produced for Picture Window Books
by Bender Richardson White, U.K.

Illustrations by James Field (pages 4–5, 9, 13, 15, 21)
and Steve Weston (cover and pages 7, 11, 17, 19).
Diagrams by Stefan Chabluk.

Photographs: iStockphoto pages 6 (Norma Cornes),
8 (Liz Leyden), 10 (Nico Smit), 12 (Jacob Hamblin),
14 (Paul Tessier), 16 (Jurie Maree), 18 (David T.
Gomez), 20 (Dawn Nichols).

Consultant: John Stidworthy, Scientific Fellow of
the Zoological Society, London, and former
Lecturer in the Education Department, Natural
History Museum, London.

## Types of dinosaurs
In this book, a red shape at the
top of a left-hand page shows
the animal was a meat-eater.
A green shape shows it was
a plant-eater.

## Just how big—or small—
were they?
Dinosaurs were many different
sizes. We have compared their
size to one of the following:

 Chicken
2 feet (60 centimeters) tall
Weight 6 pounds (2.7 kilograms)

Adult person
6 feet (1.8 meters) tall
Weight 170 pounds (76.5 kg)

 Elephant
10 feet (3 m) tall
Weight 12,000 pounds
(5,400 kg)

# TABLE OF CONTENTS

# WHAT'S INSIDE?

Dinosaurs! These dinosaurs lived in what is now the Garden Park area near the city of Denver, Colorado, in the United States. Find out how they survived millions of years ago and what they have in common with today's animals.

# LIFE IN GARDEN PARK

Dinosaurs lived between 230 million and 65 million years ago. The world did not look the same then. About halfway through the Age of Dinosaurs, the area of what is now Garden Park in the mountains of Colorado was dry plains, crisscrossed by rivers. Dinosaurs lived in and around the forests by the riversides.

A herd of long-necked
*Diplodocus* migrated across
the dry landscape to find more
plants to eat. Following them was
a pair of meat-eating *Allosaurus*.
The *Allosaurus* were stalked by a
pack of *Ceratosaurus*.

**5**

There were several types of plated dinosaurs living on the Garden Park plains. *Stegosaurus*, with its broad back plates, was the biggest. It used the plates for protection, but it may also have used them to soak up warmth from the sun.

**Sunbathers today**

A modern tuatara suns itself to warm its body, just like *Stegosaurus* once sunned itself to warm its plates.

Size Comparison

At the edge of the plains, a *Stegosaurus* caught the rays of the morning sun. Soon the dinosaur would have been warm enough to go and look for its first food of the day.

*Diplodocus* was one of the longest of the long-necked plant-eaters. It needed to keep eating all the time to feed its large body. Herds of *Diplodocus* migrated across the dry plains to find new sources of food.

**Migrating animals today**

Modern zebras migrate across the dusty landscape looking for new grazing lands, just like *Diplodocus* did long ago.

Size Comparison

Through clouds of dust, a herd of *Diplodocus* traveled from one stand of trees to another. The dry soil beneath their feet became a mass of footprints.

# COELURUS

Pronunciation:
SEE-lur-rus

Not all meat-eating dinosaurs were big. Many small ones were the size of modern foxes or jackals. *Coelurus* was one of the smallest dinosaurs of the Garden Park plains. Sometimes, *Coelurus* killed animals to eat. Other times, it ate the remains of those animals that were already dead.

**Scavengers today**

Modern jackals eat the scraps of dead animals. *Coelurus* did the same thing in dinosaur times.

Size Comparison

A pair of *Coelurus* fought over the dead body of a bigger dinosaur. There was usually plenty of food for scavengers such as *Coelurus*.

11

# ALLOSAURUS

Pronunciation:
AL-oh-SAW-rus

*Allosaurus* was the largest meat-eater of the time. It hunted the biggest of the dinosaurs, and after killing its prey, *Allosaurus* ate as much as possible. A big meal would have lasted the dinosaur for weeks.

**Big eaters today**

The modern rattlesnake does not eat often. Like *Allosaurus* once did, the rattlesnake takes in enough food at one time to keep it going for days.

Size Comparison

An *Allosaurus* rested after eating from an *Apatosaurus* that it had recently killed. The *Allosaurus* was full, and it would not eat again for weeks.

# CERATOSAURUS

Pronunciation:
Si-RAT-uh-SAW-rus

*Ceratosaurus* was one of the medium-sized meat-eating dinosaurs. It hunted by ambush, hiding and waiting for suitable prey to come along. When an animal did show up, *Ceratosaurus* would leap out and kill it.

**Surprise attacks today**

Just like *Ceratosaurus once* did, modern alligators wait, ready to attack when their prey comes near.

Size Comparison

14

In the undergrowth, a *Ceratosaurus* watched a herd of *Apatosaurus*. *Ceratosaurus* was waiting until it could leap out and catch one of them by surprise.

15

# APATOSAURUS

Pronunciation:
a-PAT-o-SAW-rus

*Apatosaurus* was a big, heavy, long-necked plant-eater. It was so big that other animals, like the pterosaurs, flew around it, catching the insects that were disturbed as it moved along. The pterosaurs also settled on *Apatosaurus'* sides and pecked parasites from its skin.

### Parasite-feeders today

Modern rhinoceros are often covered in insects. Cattle egrets peck the insects off, just like the pterosaurs did to *Apatosaurus* long ago.

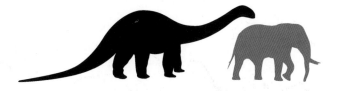

Size Comparison

An *Apatosaurus* must have enjoyed pterosaurs coming to pick off itchy insects, keeping its skin clean.

# CAMARASAURUS

Pronunciation:
KAM-uh-ruh-SAW-rus

*Camarasaurus* was the most common long-necked plant-eater of the time. Herds of *Camarasaurus* moved across the landscape, feeding as they went. They probably left nothing behind but dead undergrowth and trees stripped of their leaves.

**Herders today**

Modern elephant herds can do lots of damage to vegetation as they migrate, just as herds of *Camarasaurus* once did.

Size Comparison

A *Camarasaurus* needed an enormous amount of food. Its body was much bigger than that of a modern elephant.

# BRACHIOSAURUS

The tallest dinosaur of the ancient Garden Park plains was *Brachiosaurus*. With a neck long enough to reach into a modern building's fifth-floor window, it ate leaves from the highest trees.

## Tall feeders today

On the plains of Africa, modern giraffes feed from high tree branches, just as *Brachiosaurus* once did.

Size Comparison

Long-necked plant-eaters like *Brachiosaurus* ate all of the twigs and leaves from the lower levels of tall trees.

21

# Where Did They Go?

Dinosaurs are extinct, which means that none of them are alive today. Scientists study rocks and fossils to find clues about what happened to dinosaurs.

People have different explanations about what happened. Some people think a huge asteroid that hit Earth caused all sorts of climate changes, which caused the dinosaurs to die. Others think volcanic eruptions caused the climate change and that killed the dinosaurs. No one knows for sure what happened to all of the dinosaurs.

# Glossary

**herd**—a large group of animals that moves, feeds, and sleeps together

**migrate**—to move from place to place in search of food or shelter or to mate and bring up young

**parasite**—an animal (or plant) that lives in or on another creature and depends on it for food

**plains**—large areas of flat land with few large plants

**prey**—an animal that is hunted and eaten for food

**pterosaur**—a flying reptile related to dinosaurs

**scavenger**—an animal that takes and eats prey killed by other animals

# To Learn More

## More Books to Read

Clark, Neil, and William Lindsay. *1001 Facts About Dinosaurs.* New York: Dorling Kindersley, 2002.

Dixon, Dougal. *Dougal Dixon's Amazing Dinosaurs.* Honesdale, Penn.: Boyds Mills Press, 2007.

Holtz, Thomas R. and Michael Brett-Surman. *Jurassic Park Institute Dinosaur Field Guide.* New York: Random House, 2001.

## On the Web

FactHound offers a safe, fun way to find Web sites related to topics in this book. All of the sites on FactHound have been researched by our staff.

1. Visit *www.facthound.com*

2. Type in this special code: 1404847170

3. Click on the FETCH IT button.

Your trusty FactHound will fetch the best Web sites for you!

# Index

## Look for other books in the Dinosaur Find series:

Bambiraptor and Other Feathered Dinosaurs

Baryonyx and Other Dinosaurs of the Isle of Wight Digs in England

Camarasaurus and Other Dinosaurs of the Garden Park Digs in Colorado

Chungkingosaurus and Other Plated Dinosaurs

Deinocheirus and Other Big, Fierce Dinosaurs

Diceratops and Other Horned Dinosaurs

Pawpawsaurus and Other Armored Dinosaurs

Torosaurus and Other Dinosaurs of the Badlands Digs in Montana

Tsintaosaurus and Other Duck-billed Dinosaurs

Xiaosaurus and Other Dinosaurs of the Dashanpu Digs in China